INDONESIA

TRISTAN BURTON

Evans

TITLES IN THE COUNTRIES OF THE WORLD SERIES:

ARGENTINA • AUSTRALIA • BRAZIL • CANADA • CHILE
CHINA • EGYPT • FRANCE • GERMANY • INDIA • INDONESIA
ITALY • JAPAN • KENYA • MEXICO • NIGERIA • POLAND
RUSSIA • SOUTH KOREA • SPAIN • SWEDEN • UNITED KINGDOM
USA • VIETNAM

Published by Evans Brothers Limited
2A Portman Mansions
Chiltern Street
London W1U 6NR

VISIT OUR WEBSITE
Evans
www.evansbooks.co.uk

First published 2006
© copyright Evans Brothers 2006

Produced for Evans Brothers Limited by
Monkey Puzzle Media Limited
Gissing's Farm, Fressingfield
Suffolk IP21 5SH, UK

British Library Cataloguing in Publication Data
Burton, Tristan
Indonesia. – (Countries of the world)
1. Indonesia – Juvenile literature
I.Title
959.8'039

ISBN 0 237 52853 3
13-digit ISBN (from 1 January 2007) 978 0 237 52853 9

Editor: Clare Weaver
Designer: Mayer Media Ltd
Picture research: Lynda Lines and Frances Bailey
Map artwork by Peter Bull
Charts and graph artwork by Encompass Graphics Ltd

Endpapers (front): Friday prayers at the
Istiqlal Mesid in Jakarta. It is the largest
mosque in Indonesia.
Title page: Buyers and sellers at a market in
Denpasar, Bali.
Imprint and Contents pages: Boats at the jetty
on Gili Trawangan, a small island off Lombok.
Endpapers (back): Irrigated rice terraces, Bali.

Picture acknowledgements
Photographs were kindly supplied by the following: Alamy front cover
upper middle (Peter Bowater); Corbis 15 top, 17 (Michael Freeman), 23
(Michael Freeman), 24 (Nik Wheeler), 55 (Kaveh Kazemi); Empics 22
(EPA); Eye Ubiquitous/Hutchison front cover lower middle (Bennett
Dean), 14 (Stuart Wilson), 19 (Tim Motion), 35 (Jeremy Horner), 48
(Paul Seheult); Getty Images 11 top (Agus Suparto/AFP), 11 bottom
(Paul Chesley/Stone), 12 (Bay Ismoyo/AFP), 13 (Edy Purnomo), 20 (Adek
Berry/AFP), 27 (Choo Youn-Kong/AFP), 29 (Paula Bronstein), 36 (AFP),
43 (Dimas Ardian), 49 (Tim Laman/National Geographic), 52 (Bay
Ismoyo/AFP), 53 (Bay Ismoyo/AFP), 57 (Jewel Samad/AFP), back
endpapers (Denis Waugh/Stone); Mark Henley front endpapers, 10,
26, 32, 34, 38, 44; Image State 51 (Anup Shah); Panos Pictures 41
(Rob Huibers); Edward Parker/Images Everything Ltd 8 top, 33, 56;
Photolibrary.com 25 (David Ball); Reuters 31 (Darren Whiteside), 37
(Beawiharta), 40 (Beawiharta), 42, 45; Rex Features front cover top
(MAI), 28 (SIPA), 61 (Eye Ubiquitous); Still Pictures front cover bottom
(Russell Gordon), 5 (Mark Edwards), 8 bottom (Johann Schneibner),
18 (Adrian Arbib), 30 (Ron Giling), 46 (Alain Compost), 47 (Alain
Compost), 50 (Mark Edwards); Thames Water Asia/PT Thames Pam
Jaya 39; Thirdangle.com 6–7; Topfoto.co.uk 16, 54 (Edy Purnomo/
The Image Bank).

CONTENTS

The colours of the
Indonesian flag represent
palm-sugar (red),
and rice (white).

INTRODUCING INDONESIA

Famed for its beaches and coral reefs, Indonesia also has much more to offer.

Indonesia in South-east Asia is the world's largest archipelago (group of islands). The 17,508 islands stretch from the Indian to the Pacific Oceans, crossing the Equator and bridging the continents of Asia and Australasia. It has the world's fourth largest population – 212 million – and the largest Muslim population of any country in the world. It is a country with an amazing diversity of landscapes, people and wildlife.

Indonesia shares 2,830km of land borders with Malaysia, East Timor and Papua New Guinea. It reaches around 5,150km from east to west, and 2,012km from north to south. Volcanoes form the backbone to the country, running down from Sumatra through to Nusa Tengarra, before looping round through

Maluku and Sulawesi. It is one of the most volcanically active countries in the world, forming part of the Pacific Ring-of-Fire (see page 14).

A YOUNG NATION

Inhabiting 6,000 of the archipelago's islands, the people of Indonesia are diverse, with over

A *gamelan* orchestra on Bali. *Gamelan* is the traditional form of Indonesian music.

300 different ethnic groups, and more than 350 languages. However, they all form one nation, with one main official language of Bahasa Indonesian. For over 300 years the Dutch ruled the islands, then known as the Dutch East Indies, and Indonesia only gained independence from the Netherlands in 1949.

Indonesia remains a country of contrasts. There are vast differences between the islands. Papua has a population density of only 6 people per square kilometre, compared to the island of Java, which makes up only 7 per cent of the total land area, but has a staggering 59 per cent of the population. The government has tried to move people from Java to the other islands, but this has sometimes led to violence between different ethnic communities. There are many inequalities within Indonesia, between the rich and the poor, and between urban and rural areas. Although poverty is declining it is still a major problem, which needs to be solved. Many aspects of daily life are gradually getting better for people in Indonesia, but there is still a long way to go.

Indonesia has a wealth of natural resources, including oil, gas and coal, metals and forest products. It is unique in its diversity of Asian and Australian plants and animals. The challenge facing Indonesia is how to develop its economy while at the same time protecting its environment. Industrial pollution, illegal logging, poaching and the destruction of habitats are some of the major environmental problems threatening Indonesia today.

KEY DATA

Official Name:	Republic of Indonesia
Area:	1,919,440km^2
Population:	211,559,000 (2000 Census)
Official Language:	Bahasa Indonesian
Main Cities:	Jakarta (Java) (capital), Surabaya (Java), Bandung (Java), Medan (Sumatra), Semarang (Java), Palembang (Sumatra)
GDP Per Capita:	US$3,361*
Currency:	Rupiah
Exchange Rate:	US$1 = 9,664 rupiah £1 = 17,575 rupiah

*(2003) Calculated on Purchasing Power Parity basis
Source: World Bank

INDONESIA'S ISLANDS AND MAJOR CITIES

HISTORY OF INDONESIA UP TO 1945

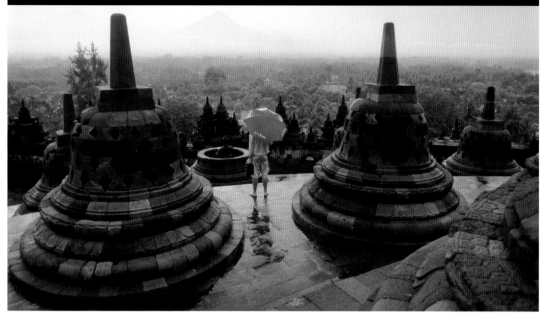

The spectacular Buddhist monument of Borobudur in Java, built between AD 750–850.

Little is known about the development of humans on the Indonesian islands. In 1891, a Dutch doctor, Eugene Dubois, discovered fossils of a human ancestor, whom he called Java Man. Java Man is an example of *Homo erectus* (an ancestor of modern humans).

PRE-HISTORY

Samples found in Indonesia range in age from 40,000 to 1.7 million years ago. Modern humans (*Homo sapiens*) arrived some 60,000 years ago, so the two species existed at the same time for many thousands of years.

The first settlers in Indonesia are believed to have been descended from Malay (Southeast Asian) and Austro-Melanesian (New Guinea) people. Around 3,000 years ago the Dongson culture, which began in what is now Vietnam and southern China, spread to the archipelago. This marked the beginning of wet-rice cultivation, which has been especially important in Java and Bali.

EARLY KINGDOMS

Hinduism and Buddhism began to arrive from India around the second century AD, spreading throughout the main islands. Trade was beginning to flourish between India, China and the Middle East and early kingdoms began to form throughout the archipelago. The Hindu-Buddhist Sriwijaya kingdom on the Sumatran coast grew up around this international trade in the seventh century. In central Java, early kingdoms developed around organised agriculture between the eighth and tenth centuries.

The Majaphit kingdom in the thirteenth century was the first to gain control over much of the archipelago. At this time, more traders from the Middle East were arriving and they started to form larger communities. Islam began to spread along the trade routes and by the sixteenth century it had become the major religion throughout the islands. However, Hinduism remained the dominant religion in some places, such as Bali, and for some people, like the Tengger in east Java.

In 2004, one of the most exciting scientific discoveries of recent years was found on the Indonesian island of Flores. In a limestone cave, scientists found a complete skeleton, along with several bones and teeth from other individuals. The remains were of a new species of hominid (relatives of human beings) called *Homo floresiensis*. These people measured about 1m tall, with a brain one third the size of modern humans (*Homo sapiens*). Tests on the bones estimated they were 18,000 years old – this means that these people lived at the same time as modern humans for thousands of years. Indonesian legends talk of small peoples living in the forests even today.

Scientists compare the small skull of *Homo floresiensis* with the skull of modern humans.

COLONIALISM

European countries were also expanding trade and their power throughout the world. The Portuguese were the first Europeans to arrive in Indonesia in the sixteenth century, looking to dominate the lucrative spice trade.

However, it was the Dutch, through the United East Indies Company, who established power in the islands and took complete control of the spice trade. In 1799, the Dutch government took direct control of the region from the trading company. It established the Dutch East Indies as part of the Dutch empire, with its capital in Batavia (now Jakarta). Dutch rule continued until the Second World War and the Japanese invasion of Indonesia in 1942.

Spices remain important agricultural products in Indonesia today.

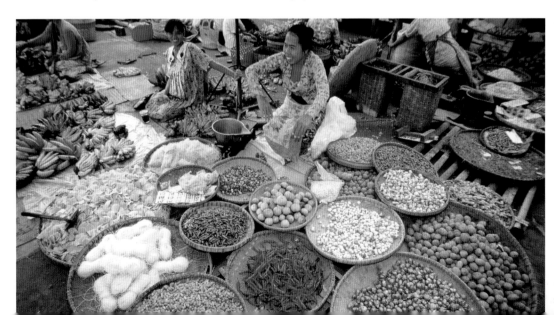

MODERN HISTORY AND POLITICS

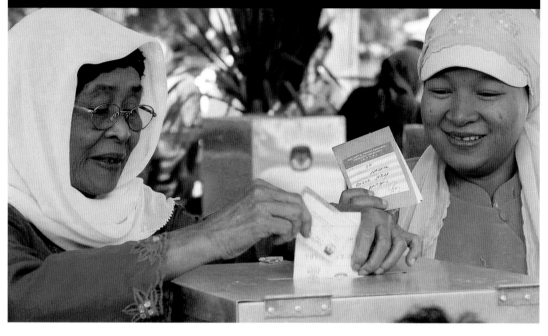

Muslim women vote in the first direct presidential elections in 2004.

By the Second World War, many Indonesians were becoming unhappy with being ruled over by foreign powers, and wanted independence. On 17 August 1945, two days after the Japanese surrendered, the Indonesian nationalist movement, led by Sukarno and Mohammad Hatta, declared independence from the Dutch. The Dutch returned to claim their colony and bitter fighting raged, alongside United Nations-led attempts at resolution. On 27 December 1949, power was officially handed over, except for Papua, which the Dutch retained until 1963.

INDEPENDENCE AND PRESIDENT SUKARNO

Sukarno became the first president of the new Republic of Indonesia in 1950. Democracy was plagued with political divisions and regional rebellions in this early period. To try and increase political stability, Sukarno introduced a new system of rule called Guided Democracy. Sukarno and the cabinet took more control, limiting the say of parliament and the people. With Sukarno moving closer towards the Indonesian Communist Party (called the PKI) – which was the third largest in the world after the Soviet Union and China – the military felt they were losing their political power.

SUHARTO – 30 YEARS OF RULE

On 30 September 1965, there was an attempted coup (take-over of power) by dissident officers. General Suharto seized the initiative – he took control of the armed forces and blamed the coup on the PKI. There was a purge of anyone suspected of being a communist. Between 160,000 and 500,000 people are reported to have died in these attacks. Sukarno's political position became very weak and Suharto gradually took power.

The PKI was banned and Suharto became president in 1968.

Suharto set about creating a so called New Order, where expanding the economy had central importance. Life improved for many people, but corruption was a major problem, with the friends and family of Suharto making huge fortunes. Any challenges to Suharto's authoritarian rule were crushed and he remained president for 30 years. The end of Suharto began with the Asian economic crisis in 1997, made worse by falling oil prices and widespread drought. Pro-democracy demonstrations led by students, rioting over rising prices and power struggles within the military eventually gave Suharto no option but to resign on 21 May 1998.

POLITICAL REFORM AND DEMOCRACY

Vice-President B.J. Habibie replaced Suharto, and called the first national elections in 1999 – a major move towards political reform after almost four decades of authoritarian rule. Abdurrahman Wahid became president, but was ousted, being replaced by Megawati Sukarnoputri – the daughter of former president Sukarno. In September 2004, Susilo Bambang Yudhoyono became the first president to be directly elected by the Indonesian people. He has promised to fight corruption, rejuvenate the economy and tackle separatist conflict.

CASE STUDY
EAST TIMOR

In 1975, East Timor gained independence from the Portuguese. Suharto feared East Timor would be influenced by communists, leading to separatist rebellions in Indonesia. So, in December 1975, Indonesian armed forces invaded the country, and East Timor became a province of Indonesia in 1976. During this period it is estimated between 100,000 and 200,000 East Timorese died from violence or famine.

In 1999, East Timorese were given a referendum on their future and voted for independence. Pro-Indonesian militia began a campaign of terror throughout the region. United Nations (UN) peacekeeping forces arrived to regain order. With UN assistance, East Timor gained independence from Indonesia in May 2002, but the transition has not been easy as poverty remains high and security is still a concern.

East Timorese celebrate independence in May 2002.

Landscape and Climate

Mount Bromo is highly significant to the Hindu Tengger people of Java.

From the white sandy beaches to the smoking volcanic craters, the deep turquoise seas to the snow-capped peaks, Indonesia's spectacular landscape is one of contrasts. From the hot tropical weather of the coastal plains to the cool mountain ranges, and from flooding to droughts, the climate is equally varied across the wide-ranging islands.

THE LAND OF FIRE

Indonesia has over 400 volcanoes, of which 129 are active. A chain of volcanoes forms the backbone of Sumatra, Java, Bali and Nusa Tengarra. This then loops round through the Banda islands of Maluku, into Sulawesi. These volcanoes have been formed by the movement of tectonic plates, which make up the outer surface of Earth. The volcanoes from Sumatra to Nusa Tengarra have been formed by the Indo-Australian plate moving underneath the Eurasian plate. As one plate moves below the other – a process called subduction – the rock melts. Molten rock called magma is then forced to the surface a few hundred kilometres away, forming volcanoes.

The interaction of the tectonic plates

around Sulawesi and Maluku are more complex. Whilst Sulawesi is at the junction of the Indo-Australian and Eurasian plates; the formation of Malaku is a result of the movement of the Philippines, Eurasian and Pacific plates. Indonesia forms part of the Pacific Ring-of-Fire, a zone around the Pacific plate, which has more than half of all the volcanoes above sea level in the world.

Papua has been formed by the collision of the Indo-Australian and Pacific plates, which has forced the ground upwards over millions of years. Along with volcanoes – the highest on the island being Trikora (4,750m) – there are also glaciers. Indonesia is one of only three tropical countries in the world that have glaciers. The glacier on Punack Jaya (or Mount

CASE STUDY
THE EXPLOSION OF KRAKATAU, 1883

On 26 August 1883, one of the most famous volcanic eruptions occurred as Krakatau (sometimes called Krakatoa), a volcanic island in the Sunda Strait, exploded. Ash was sent almost 80km up into the atmosphere – plummeting people within a 250km radius into darkness. The explosion destroyed half of the island, throwing nearly 18km^3 of rock into the sky. It formed a 300 metre-deep crater underneath the ocean. The 40 metre-high tsunamis (giant waves) travelled rapidly across the oceans – reaching the African island of Madagascar ten hours later. It is estimated 36,000 people died and 165 villages were destroyed in the explosion and eruptions, which continued for two days.

Krakatau was a major world event. These drawings showing the volcano before and after the eruption were published in a London newspaper in 1883.

Jaya) – the highest mountain in Indonesia at 5,039m – is in retreat (getting smaller).

There are 65 observatories in Indonesia, monitoring 59 volcanoes. There have been many famous eruptions in Indonesia, such as Krakatau in 1883. Experts believe Lake Toba, in Sumatra, the largest lake in South-east Asia, occupies the location of a former volcano, which blasted itself away 75,000 years ago in an eruption that dwarfed Krakatau's explosion.

With such destructive power, it is no surprise most volcanoes have mythical and religious significance. Agung in Bali is considered the centre of the Balinese universe and the Tengger people make offerings to Gunung Bromo to protect them.

MAJOR VOLCANOES

ISLANDS AND SEA

There is a popular saying in Indonesia, 'Tanah Air Kita', meaning 'our earth and water'. There is more than four times as much water as land in Indonesia. The total land area is 1,919,440km^2, which is only a little larger than Queensland in Australia, but the combined areas of land and sea make Indonesia two and a half times larger than Australia.

Of the 17,508 islands, only 73 are larger than 500km^2 – about one third the size of London in the UK. Among these are three of the world's six largest islands. Papua is found on the island of New Guinea (sharing it with Papua New Guinea), which is the second largest island behind Greenland. Borneo, where the Indonesian territory of Kalimantan is found, along with Brunei and areas of Malaysia, is third. Sumatra is the sixth largest island in the world, and the largest completely Indonesian island.

The geological formation of Indonesia means the islands can be classified in three groups. First are the islands that lie on the Sunda continental shelf, including Sumatra, Borneo and Java. Papua and the Aru islands lie on the Sahal shelf. Islands found on these shelves have sea depths not exceeding 215m. Nusa Tengarra, Maluku and Sulawesi lie between the two shelves and have much greater sea depths – in some places more than 5,000m.

COASTAL PLAINS AND CORAL REEFS

The archipelago provides the ideal marine landscape for corals to grow – clear, warm and shallow water – and consequently there is a vast collection of coral reefs. Fresh water is harmful for corals, so they are found away from the mouths of rivers, but around these river estuaries and sheltered coastal plains are some of the world's most unspoilt mangrove swamps.

Many of the mountainous islands have expansive coastal plains, but some of the islands of Maluku, such as Halmahera, Seram and Buru, have steep sides rising up from the water's edge. There are very few beaches here, just rugged shorelines. Many of the smaller islands remain uninhabited, as they are simply little islands of rock, with no potential for agriculture or settlement.

THE JAVA TRENCH

About 300km off the coast of Sumatra and Java is a deep ocean trench known as the Java Trench (sometimes called the Java Deep Trench or the Sunda Trench). It runs for more than 2,600km in the Indian Ocean and can reach depths of around 7,500m. It is where the Indo-Australian tectonic plate gradually moves underneath the Eurasian plate. The edge of the Eurasian plate is much steeper than the Indo-Australian plate, which is being subducted.

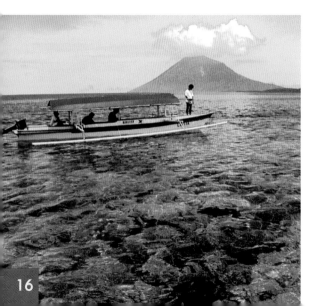

Indonesia's marine environments, such as this coral reef off Bunaken Island, Sulawesi, are some of the most important in the world.

SIZE OF MAJOR ISLANDS

New Guinea   800,311km^2 (Indonesian territory of Papua 421,981km^2)
Borneo   755,000km^2 (Indonesian territory of Kalimantan 539,460km^2)
Sumatra   473, 606km^2
Sulawesi   189,216km^2
Java   125, 622km^2
Timor   30,777km^2 (Indonesian territory of West Timor 16,510km^2)
Bali   5,561km^2

LANDSCAPE FEATURES

THE LAKES OF KELIMUTU

Near the 1,640m summit of the Kelimutu volcano three spectacular lakes can be found. The three crater lakes have different, and changing, colours. At present, the lakes are turquoise, dark brown and black. In recent years they have been blue, dark red and black. In the 1960s the colours were again different – blue, a murky red and a milky brown. It is believed the minerals from volcanic rocks cause the different water colours.

Kelimutu crater lakes on the island of Flores.

In the rainy season especially, sudden heavy downpours can cause local flooding.

CLIMATE

Indonesia has a tropical climate, which means it is warm and humid. The relative humidity is usually between 70 and 90 per cent. This can be uncomfortably sticky and explains why many Indonesians prefer to socialise in the cooler evenings. There are two main seasons, the wet – or rainy – and the dry. The wet season typically occurs between October and March. There are tropical downpours, usually in the afternoons, when a lot of rain falls in a short time. The dry season is between April and September, when temperatures are a little warmer.

Maluku is the exception to the general seasonal trends in Indonesia. In central and southern Maluku the dry season is between October and March, when the temperature averages 30°C. The wet monsoon lasts from May until August, and the temperature falls slightly to 23°C. However, in north Maluku the rainy season is from December to March, much like the rest of Indonesia.

There is a lot of variation both between islands and within different locations on the same island. The highlands in west Java average 4,000mm of rain a year, whilst on the north-east coast of Java rainfall measures only 900mm. The town of Bogor is one of the wettest places in Indonesia, with heavy rain around 322 days a year. This is over twice as many days as the capital Jakarta, which is only 60km north of Bogor. The island group of Nusa Tengarra is very dry and this is reflected in its savannah habitats, rather than the rainforests of wetter areas. The closer the island groups are to Australia, the longer the dry season tends to be, with droughts a common problem. The same islands, however, also face flooding in the rainy season as the ground cannot absorb the water fast enough.

The temperature in Indonesia varies according to the height above sea level. At low altitudes, on the coastal plains, the

PRECIPITATION

Rainfall per year (mm)

- less than 600
- 600—1,000
- 1,000—1,400
- 1,400—2,000
- 2,000—2,800
- 2,800—4,000
- 4,000—5,600

temperature averages 28°C. Inland, and at slightly higher elevations, the temperature averages a few degrees less – at 26°C. In the higher mountain regions, temperatures begin to fall further (unless you are standing on top of an active volcano!).

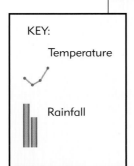

KEY:

Temperature

Rainfall

CASE STUDY
THE PALU VALLEY

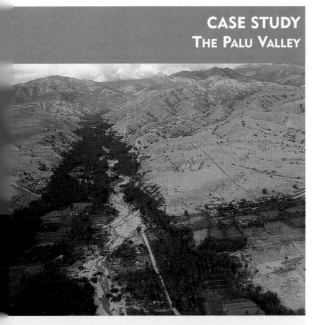

The dry Palu Valley in central Sulawesi has hot days and cooler nights.

It is reported that the Palu Valley in Sulawesi is the driest place in Indonesia with less than 500mm of rain a year. It is interesting because Palu lies only a few kilometres away from lush tropical rainforest. The winds in Sulawesi typically blow from the west, the north-west or the south-east. The valley runs from north to south. The orientation of the mountain range to the air circulation causes the rain clouds that form to deposit the water on the windward side. On the other side of the mountain – called the leeward side – very little rain falls. The Palu Valley is on the leeward side and remains very dry.

THE ECONOMY

Fixing a pipe on a tanker so oil can be shipped around the world.

Indonesia's economy was heavily dependent on the production of oil and gas until the mid-1980s, when the government began to develop other industries and manufacturing expanded. The population provided a large cheap workforce, which made Indonesian products very competitive around the world.

In the 1990s, there was a major increase in international investment. Foreign companies were arriving in Indonesia, wanting to take advantage of the large labour force and the country's ideal location for distributing products around the world. This expansion led to an increase of GDP (Gross Domestic Product) by about 8 per cent per year in the 1990s.

THE 1997 ECONOMIC CRISIS

In July 1997, the World Bank forecasted a great future for the Indonesian economy. This was soon to change as an economic crisis – starting in Thailand, before moving on to Malaysia and Indonesia – hit South-east Asia. In July 1997 US$1 was worth 2,600 rupiah. Throughout the economic crisis the value of the currency rapidly declined. It eventually stabilised in 1998 – at around 10,000 rupiah to US$1. At its lowest point, one dollar could buy 17,000 rupiah. This was a disaster for the economy. International companies quickly withdrew billions of dollars to save their investments. Local companies were in trouble. Many had borrowed money from overseas and had to pay it back in US dollars – yet they earned rupiah, which now was worth much less. Many Indonesians lost their businesses and the number of people living below the poverty line increased.

THE ECONOMY TODAY

Following the crisis, the Indonesian economy shrunk. Today, it is growing again, but at a much slower rate than in the 1990s. The amount of money the government owes from borrowing, called the national debt, is US$130.8 billion. The major industries in Indonesia today are the manufacturing of paper and pulp, cement and fertilizers; the extraction of basic metals, power generation, telecommunications and transport. The country is a major exporter of textiles, garments and shoes; oil and gas; electrical goods and wood products. Indonesia's main imports are chemicals and pharmaceuticals, cotton yarns and fabrics used in the textile industry, motor vehicles and industrial

MAJOR TRADING PARTNERS (% OF VALUE), 2003

EXPORTS

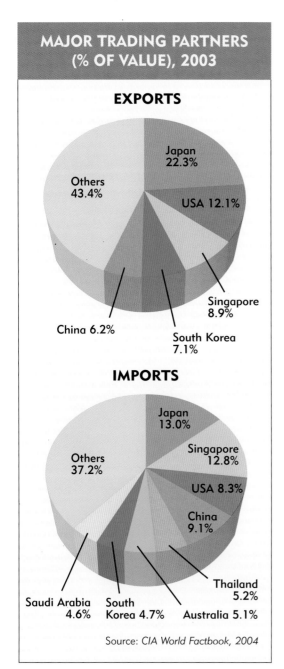

IMPORTS

Source: *CIA World Factbook, 2004*

GNI PER CAPITA (US$)

Source: World Bank

ELECTRICITY PRODUCTION BY SOURCE

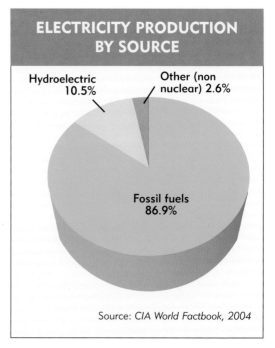

Source: *CIA World Factbook, 2004*

machinery. The service industries – including tourism, banking, health and education – are also growing.

OIL AND GAS

Indonesia is amongst the top ten producers of natural gas in the world, having reserves of 2.549 trillion cubic metres. Of the 69 billion cubic metres produced each year, 32.8 billion cubic metres are exported. Indonesia is the world's biggest producer of liquefied natural gas (LNG). This is a process by which natural gas is converted into a liquid form, reducing its volume by 600 times, so making it easier to transport overseas. At the end of its journey, LNG is returned to its natural gaseous state by reheating it. Indonesia is also a major oil producer – averaging 1.2 million barrels per day. In 1990, gas and oil accounted for 43.1 per cent of export earnings, but this fell to 21.1 per cent in 2003 as the manufacturing and service sectors expanded.

MINING

Indonesia has a wealth of mining potential. Large areas of the archipelago have not been surveyed yet, so the full possibilities are not known. However, the sector is in crisis. In 1999, in a move to safeguard the environment, the government banned open-cast mining in protected forested areas. Many large companies had already signed contracts with the government to develop projects in these areas. This uncertainty has meant investment in mining has drastically declined since 1999. To try and boost the sector, the government permitted 13 companies with operations in place to continue, and 9 more with exploration contracts to restart work, in May 2004.

Coal, however, is one of the few growth mining industries in Indonesia. In 2003, Indonesia extracted 109.3 million tonnes, an increase of 6.3 million tonnes from 2002. Of this, 70 per cent is exported. Indonesia has the world's largest coal mine in north-east Kalimantan, run by Kaltim Prima Coal (KPC). The KPC mine makes US$450 million per year from coal exports.

Gold and silver are two precious metals mined in Indonesia. From 1983 to 2001 the production of gold increased by over 70 times, from 2,340kg to 166,100kg. In the same period, silver increased almost 10 times. Since 2001, the amount of both silver and gold produced has declined slightly. Part of the reason for this is local opposition to mines. In 2003, a gold mine in Halmaherra, Malaku – run by an Australian company, Gold Crest – was occupied by demonstrators who disrupted mining operations. Many people feel the profits of mining are not put back into local communities. Instead, they often face relocation, loss of land and pollution problems created by the mines.

Indonesia is also a leading supplier of tin – with estimated deposits of 1 million tonnes. Nickel is another metallic element in abundance – 4.4 million tonnes were mined in 2003.

Indonesia has 500 million tonnes of bauxite reserves. The government and the Japanese Overseas Economic Cooperation Fund jointly funded an aluminium smelting plant in north Sumatra in 1985. The plant processes the bauxite for aluminium production, which has increased from 808,749 tonnes in 1997, to 1.3 million tonnes in 2003.

Environmental groups believe that open-cast mining in protected forest areas will have devastating consequences.

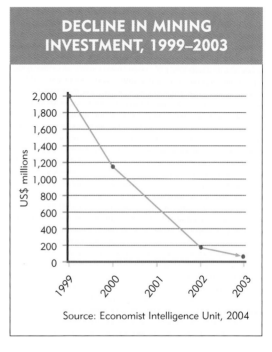

DECLINE IN MINING INVESTMENT, 1999–2003

US$ millions

Source: Economist Intelligence Unit, 2004

The Grasberg open-cast mine in Papua is the second largest copper mine and the largest gold mine in the world. From copper alone, the mine is estimated to make US$1 million a day. It is run by Freeport Indonesia, part of the US-owned Freeport McMoRan company. It employs 18,000 people, but only about 30 per cent are Papuan – the rest come from other parts of Indonesia or are foreign workers. Although the company spends money on community development, many feel this is inadequate compensation for the relocation of villages caused by the mine.

Freeport McMoRan admitted to paying the Indonesian armed forces US$5.6 million in 2002 for security services. The company and the Indonesian armed forces have been criticised for alleged brutality against protestors. Protests have focused around the destruction of over 30,000 hectares of rainforest and damage to rivers. Local indigenous groups claim to have lost ancestral lands.

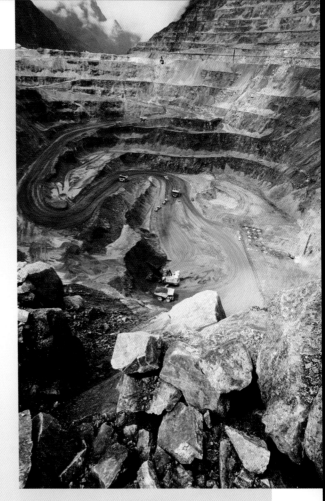

The Grasberg mine remains controversial for its destruction of forest and ancestral lands.

MINERALS, OIL AND GAS

Oil and gas

Coal

Gold

Tin

Other minerals

Aceh

BRUNEI

Celebes Sea

PACIFIC OCEAN

Nias

M A L A Y S I A

SINGAPORE

Sumatra

Equator

Kalimantan

Maluku

I N D O N E S I A

Sulawesi

Seram

Papua

PAPUA NEW GUINEA

Grasberg mine

INDIAN OCEAN

Java

Nusa Tengarra

Lombok

Flores

Wetar

EAST TIMOR

Sumbawa

Lomblen *West Timor*

Bali

Sumba

Arafura Sea

Timor Sea

A U S T R A L I A

0   800km

0   500 miles

N

AGRICULTURE

The largest share of Indonesia's labour force – 45 per cent – works in agriculture. Although its share in the country's GDP has been declining as manufacturing and service industries have expanded, the agricultural sector has still grown. Arable land has increased from 9.9 per cent of all land in 1980, to 11.3 per cent in 2001. Similarly, permanent cropland has risen in the same period, from 4.4 to 7.2 per cent.

Indonesia is famous for rice production, especially the irrigated rice terraces of Java and Bali. It is the third largest producer of rice in the world. In 1985, the country was self-sufficient – producing enough rice for the population to eat. With transmigration, the popularity of rice has spread to islands where historically other foods, like cassava, formed the staple crop. With population growth as well, Indonesia has needed to import rice since 1985. However, with increasing rice cultivation, the government announced

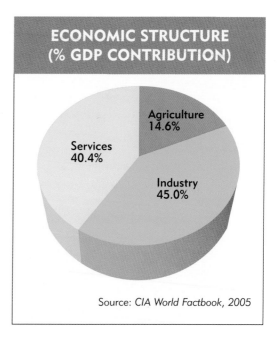

ECONOMIC STRUCTURE (% GDP CONTRIBUTION)

- Agriculture 14.6%
- Services 40.4%
- Industry 45.0%

Source: *CIA World Factbook, 2005*

Indonesia was again self-sufficient in rice at the end of 2004.

Spices have been historically important to the islands. During the colonial period, mace (the outer covering of nutmeg, used as a spice) was more expensive than its weight in gold. Although the spice trade is not as important as it once was, it still earns Indonesia over US$186 million a year. It is the largest producer of nutmeg and second only to India in pepper production.

The cultivation of coffee and cocoa is increasing as plantations expand. Indonesia is the largest producer of the Robusta coffee bean, earning US$218.8 million in 2002, and the second largest cocoa producer behind Côte d'Ivoire. Rubber, another plantation crop, earns Indonesia around US$1.5 billion a year.

Oil-palm cultivation is a rapidly expanding agricultural product. In 2002, almost 10 million tonnes of crude palm oil (CPO) were produced on large plantations, employing some 2 million people.

LEFT: Nutmeg pickers on the Banda Islands. When the fruit is ripe it splits, revealing the nutmeg.

Wet-rice cultivation requires vast amounts of water. For centuries, the terrace rice farmers of Bali have arranged access to water at local water temples. The farmers make offerings to the gods and goddesses, and the water priests bless the crop. The water priests are responsible for making sure each farmer has a fair share of the water, and they sort out all disputes.

In the 1970s, the Indonesian government wanted to modernise agricultural production. By using new fertilisers and pesticides, farmers were encouraged to grow more rice. The water priests no longer controlled the allocation of water. More water was used in the new system and, at first, there was an increase in rice yields. This did not last – shortages of water became a problem, and the rice crop became infested by pests.

The rice farmers wanted to go back to the traditional system. The government was opposed to this as the system of water allocation was not scientifically proven. In 1987, an American scientist developed a computer model of the Balinese agricultural system. It demonstrated the sharing of water by the priests was ecologically successful. Faced with this scientific explanation the government backed down, and the water priests are again in control.

The major Balinese water temple of Ulun Danu, which controls the vast water resources of Lake Batur for rice farmers.

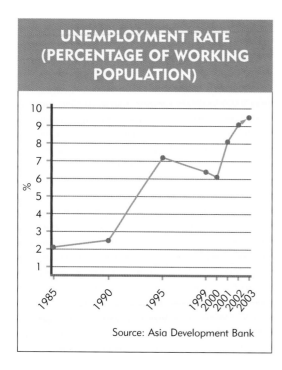

UNEMPLOYMENT RATE (PERCENTAGE OF WORKING POPULATION)

Source: Asia Development Bank

FISHERIES

The seas surrounding Indonesia are a major source of income for the country. In 2002, exported shrimp brought over $840 million into the country. Fish and other marine products, excluding shrimp, were worth US$378 million in the same year. These figures have the potential to be higher, as illegal fishing in Indonesian waters is a problem. Though the government is now cracking down on illegal boats, there is still a loss of revenue of up to US$1 billion and a decline in the fish stocks.

MANUFACTURING
FOREST PRODUCTS

The vast forests of Indonesia are a valuable natural resource, and have made the country the largest exporter of forest products in

Hardwoods arrive in Jakarta from Kalimantan for use in the construction industry.

Changes in world trade threaten many jobs in the textile industry.

South-east Asia. Revenue from forest products has fallen since the economic crisis, as there was less demand by construction, and logging quotas were reduced to stop the over-exploitation of the forests. There is a vast illegal trade of logging and smuggling, estimated to be worth US$7.2 billion – compared to official trade valued around US$3.2 billion a year.

Plywood production, centred in Kalimantan (along with pulp and paper manufacturing), has been criticised for exceeding logging quotas. By the end of 1999, there were 88 paper mills with a capacity to produce 10.7 million tonnes of paper each year. To reach these maximum levels 25 million cubic metres of timber were required. However, as only 3.5 million cubic metres were available to the industry, much of the shortfall was made up of illegally logged trees.

TEXTILES

The textile, garment and footwear industry provides the second largest income from overseas exports after oil and gas, with a value of around US$10 billion per year. Cotton is imported for use in garments but, with its abundance of petrochemicals, Indonesia is able to produce nylon, polyester and other synthetic fabrics for use.

The textile industry – the largest employer of female labour in the manufacturing sector – is under serious threat. In 2002, 242 companies went bankrupt. Many companies could not compete with lower labour costs in countries such as Vietnam and Cambodia. The situation is set to worsen. Indonesia's textile industry has been protected by import quotas in the USA and Europe. These quotas are set to disappear in 2005, and Indonesia will not be able to compete with large-scale producers like India and China that have cheaper labour.

CEMENT AND OTHER PRODUCTS

The production of cement is an important industry in Indonesia, supplying both the domestic and international markets. During the economic boom years of the 1980s and early 1990s, the construction (building) industry expanded, so increasing the need for cement production. In 2001, 8 million tonnes was exported, with a value of US$161 million. In 2002, cement exports fell, as the construction industry in Indonesia began to grow – consequently requiring more cement for domestic use.

Machinery and electrical appliances provide the third largest earnings from exports. This reached an all-time high of US$10.3 billion in 2000, declining to US$8.6 billion in 2001.

TOURISM

Tourism is an expanding service industry in Indonesia. In 1993, just over 3.4 million people visited Indonesia – rising to a peak of almost 5.2 million in 1997. Following the riots and violence in May 1998 (see pages 12–13), fewer tourists visited the country, but from 1999 to 2002, tourist numbers rose again. Australians are the most frequent tourists to the islands, making up 27 per cent of international visitors.

The end of 2002 saw the beginning of a troubled year for tourism in Indonesia. The fear of terrorism, following the Bali bombings in October, reduced the numbers arriving. This was then followed by the outbreak of SARS (severe acute respiratory syndrome), which kept large numbers of visitors away from the whole of

CASE STUDY
THE BALI BOMBINGS

On 12 October 2002, a bomb exploded in the popular tourist destination of Kuta on Bali. The bomb blasted through clubs and bars, injuring well over 300 people and killing 202. People of 23 different nationalities died in the bomb blast, the most being Indonesian and Australian. Another bomb also exploded near the US consulate in Sanur, near Kuta, without causing injury or death.

The effect on tourism was immediate – international governments issued warnings against travelling to Indonesia in case of further attacks. The monthly numbers of tourists arriving fell dramatically – from 150,747 in September to 31,498 in November. The attacks were linked to an Islamic extremist organisation called Jemaah Islamiah. In August 2003, four suspects were sentenced for the bombings. Three were given the death penalty.

Police investigate the bombing of a nightclub in Kuta in October 2002.

Main road
Railway
International airport

South-east Asia and China. Tourist-related businesses found it difficult to make money, and unemployment levels increased – but by the end of 2003 and the beginning of 2004 tourist numbers were again starting to grow.

Indonesia is a very popular place to go snorkelling and scuba diving, but these activities can damage the marine habitat. The growth of eco-tourism should help to encourage protection of the environment and provide a good source of income for local communities. The diversity of Indonesian peoples and their rich traditions provide an opportunity to expand cultural tourism. Cultural tourism allows visitors to see, learn and appreciate different ideas and ways of living.

TRANSPORT AND COMMUNICATIONS

The Strait of Malacca, which lies between Malaysia and Indonesia, see one-quarter of all maritime trade in the world. Some 50,000 ships a year pass through the channel, which is only one and a half nautical miles wide at its narrowest point. In 2003, 27 per cent of the world's illegal attacks on ships occurred here, posing a potential environmental hazard as many vessels using the Strait are taking oil to Japan, China and South Korea.

Ferries and other boats link the islands in the archipelago. River travel in Indonesia is not widespread as the rivers are often too narrow or too shallow for larger boats. Kalimantan, with its extensive water networks is the exception, and boats are used to access the more remote areas. Road building is increasing throughout the archipelago – Indonesia has over 340,000km of highway – though future road building plans threaten to pass through important ecological areas.

Indonesia is famous for its beaches and surfing, attracting people from all over the world.

A busy street scene in Bandung, central Java. Indonesia's large population contains many ethnic groups.

I ndonesia is a hugely diverse nation with many different peoples and cultures. This is summed up well by its national motto – *bhinneka tunggal ika* – meaning 'unity in diversity' or 'they are many, they are one'. This diversity does cause pressures at times but, for the most part, Indonesians manage to live peacefully together.

ETHNIC DIVERSITY

There are over 300 different ethnic groups in Indonesia, speaking over 350 different languages. The languages can be divided into two main groups – Malay and Papuan. The Malay languages (over 200) are related to those on mainland South-east Asia, and originate from the Malay ancestors who first spread through the islands from west to east. The 150 Papuan languages reflect the people first arriving in the east of the archipelago. The island of New Guinea (Papua of Indonesia and the separate country of Papua New Guinea) accounts for 15 per cent of all the known languages in the world.

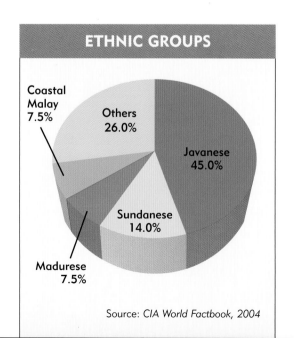

ETHNIC GROUPS

- Coastal Malay 7.5%
- Others 26.0%
- Javanese 45.0%
- Sundanese 14.0%
- Madurese 7.5%

Source: *CIA World Factbook, 2004*

FUNERAL CEREMONIES OF THE TORAJA

The Toraja on Sulawesi have elaborate funeral ceremonies called the *tomate* – if not carried out, the soul of the deceased will bring misfortune to the family. The first funeral is immediately after the death. The body is preserved and remains in the house whilst arrangements are made for the grand second funeral. This can take months, and depends on the time of the year, as people wait for the dry season. The ceremony involves animal sacrifices, dancing, singing and eating and can last several days.

Some ethnic groups, like the Badui and the Kubu, remained isolated from the outside world as trade began to develop. Others, like the Balinese and Javanese, have had a long history of contact with outsiders. Many groups have a history of moving around territories as they cultivated new areas for food and allowed old areas to regenerate. The changing economy means many ethnic groups have lost their ancestral lands and have had to settle in permanent communities. The Bajo people traditionally lived on the seas, travelling between Indonesia, Malaysia and the Philippines. The Bajo still dive for sea cucumbers, pearls and other sea products, but also have settled communities on the mainland.

The Javanese make up the largest ethnic group in Indonesia (45 per cent), but Bahasa Indonesian became the national language, not Javanese. This was important for Indonesia when it gained independence, as it gave the crucial message that all the islands, not just Java, were of equal importance.

The Chinese have been trading on the Indonesian islands for centuries. In the seventeenth century, only men were allowed to migrate from China. Some of these Chinese men settled on the islands and married local women. Children with a Chinese father and Indonesian mother were known as Chinese Peranakans. When they grew up, they tended to marry other Chinese Peranakans, so a new ethnic group was formed. Over the generations, Bahasa Indonesian has become their first language, with Chinese second. Unlike similar groups in Malaysia (the Babas) – and in the Philippines (Mestizos) – the Peranakans have remained a distinct group within Indonesia, accounting for almost 3 per cent of the population.

Traditional Peranakan dress worn during a festival following the Chinese New Year.

POPULATION TRENDS

Indonesia has the world's fourth largest population behind China, India and the USA. Since the 1950s, the population has increased by 2.7 times, from just over 79.5 million people to almost 212 million in 2000.

Under President Sukarno's leadership, families were encouraged to have as many children as possible. This was part of a programme to provide a large workforce, which would enable Indonesian industry to compete with the rest of the world, bringing money and development to the country. The expansion was aimed at increasing the number of people and industries on those islands that had smaller populations.

When Suharto came to power the population programme was reversed. People were encouraged to plan the size of their families – to help reduce the growth in the population. This was focused especially in areas with high populations, such as Java and Bali. It was reported that 80 per cent of people using the Family Planning Services were from poorer families, who tended traditionally to have larger families. Many people, especially in Java, believe the saying '*dua anak cukup*', which means 'two children are enough'.

The sizes of families continue to be larger in areas with strong Muslim communities. Parents in rural areas also often have more children than those in urban areas. This acts as 'insurance' for the parents in old age, making sure someone is there to look after them and their land. Overall, in Indonesia there has been a decline in the birth rate in recent years – this means that less people are being born each year. However, more people are being born than the number of people dying, so the population is still increasing. It is estimated that, over the next 20 years, Indonesia's population will increase on average by about 2 million a year.

The size of families is declining, especially within major urban areas.

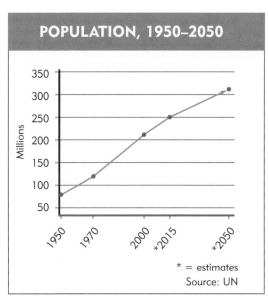

POPULATION, 1950–2050

Millions

* = estimates
Source: UN

Children in a mangrove fishing village, Kalimantan.

POPULATION STRUCTURE

Every ten years the government takes a census, which includes lots of information about the population. This was last carried out in 2000. The structure of the population is one such piece of information. There are only slightly more men in Indonesia than women. Also, 30 per cent of the population was under the age of 15, and more than half was under the age of 25. This is very different from the population structure of the UK, for example, which has a much smaller percentage of the population below these ages. With such a large percentage of young people, there are pressures on the government to provide enough social and welfare services – such as education and immunization programmes. With the declining birth rates and increasing life expectancy, the structure will have changed by the next census in 2010. There will be a smaller percentage of young people in the population. In the next decade unemployment could be a major problem. More jobs will need to be created to meet the growing population reaching working age, or unemployment and poverty will increase.

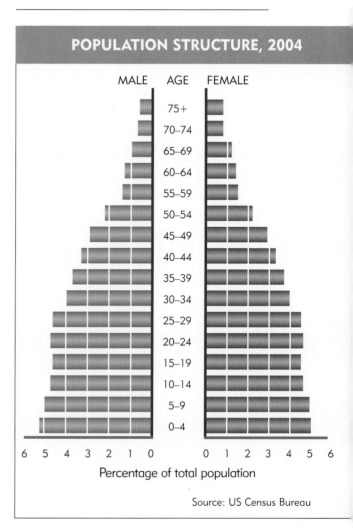

POPULATION STRUCTURE, 2004

MALE   AGE   FEMALE

Age
75+
70–74
65–69
60–64
55–59
50–54
45–49
40–44
35–39
30–34
25–29
20–24
15–19
10–14
5–9
0–4

6 5 4 3 2 1 0   0 1 2 3 4 5 6

Percentage of total population

Source: US Census Bureau

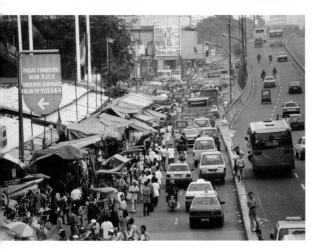

In 1971, almost 4.6 million people lived in Jakarta; in 2000, it was nearly 8.4 million.

URBANISATION AND MIGRATION

POPULATION DISTRIBUTION

The average population density of Indonesia is 109 people per square kilometre. However, the population is very unevenly distributed across the archipelago. Papua has the lowest population density, only 6 people per square kilometre, compared to Jakarta, which has the most at 12,635 people per square kilometre. The majority of the population – 59 per cent – live on the island of Java, which is less than 7 per cent of the total land area of Indonesia. This pressure on the land has resulted in attempts to redistribute the population from the densely populated areas of Java and Bali to other islands.

TRANSMIGRASI – MOVING TO THE OUTER ISLANDS

The transmigration – *transmigrasi* in Bahasa Indonesian – was started by the Dutch in 1905. It was a process of moving people away from the densely populated islands of Java and Bali to the outer islands. The Dutch moved 650,000 people, mainly from Java to Sumatra. The Indonesian government continued this policy after Independence, and it was expanded under the support of the World Bank in 1974 – believing this would diversify and strengthen the economy. Sumatra continued to be the major destination in the 1970s, but this changed to Papua (then called Irian Jaya) and Kalimantan in the 1980s. Between 1905 and 1999, 6.2 million people were moved – 3.2 million of these moved between 1984 and 1989. About two-thirds of the people have been landless peasants from rural areas.

There have been environmental and social problems associated with the transmigration policy. Forests have been cleared to create new farmland. This land has often been poorly used as people have attempted to grow unsuitable crops. Tensions have grown in some communities over the ownership and use of land (see pages 36–7). As well as these problems, the policy has been criticised for being expensive and not actually reducing the population density on Java and Bali.

URBANISATION

In the last 50 years the Indonesian population has undergone a major shift in where they live. In the 1950s, only 12 per cent of the population lived in towns and cities, now this

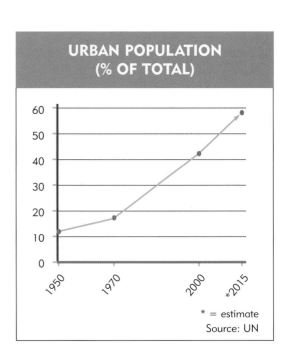

URBAN POPULATION (% OF TOTAL)

* = estimate
Source: UN

figure is reaching almost half. With the increase in manufacturing and service industries, more and more people are attracted to the cities and towns to find paid employment. Following the economic and political crisis of 1997–98, large numbers of people left the major cities. Many of the Chinese left Indonesia, as they faced violence and their businesses were looted or destroyed. Other people left to go back to rural areas. They thought they would be able to at least grow some of their own food, which was becoming too expensive for many of the poorer people in the cities. As the economy begins to grow again it is likely more people will start heading back to urban areas. Many people, unfortunately, find the cities do not offer them all the opportunities they had hoped for as they cannot find employment, do not have any land to grow their own food and have to live in cramped conditions.

POPULATION DENSITIES (PEOPLE PER km^2)

Jakarta	12,635
Java (excluding Jakarta)	927
Bali	559
Nusa Tengarra	141
Sumatra	92
Sulawesi	82
Kalimantan	30
Maluku	25
Papua	6

Source: Central Bureau of Statistics, Indonesian Census, 2000

More Indonesians are moving away from the rural areas in search of better prospects.

CONFLICT AND RECONCILIATION

Members of the Free Aceh Movement, who are fighting for independence from Indonesia.

Many people view Indonesia as a violent society. Indeed, the size and the diversity of the population do create some tensions, which have caused violent outbursts. Often, religion is blamed for conflict. In some cases, religion does play a part, but in many situations it is perhaps simply the easiest distinction for the media to make between the two sides. Conflicts arise in Indonesia for a wide range of social, cultural, political and economic reasons. However, most Indonesians live peacefully and have shown the ability to reconcile their differences in many situations.

There are some groups, such as the Free Aceh Movement and the Free Papua Movement, which want to gain independence from Indonesia. They are known as separatist groups and have been fighting with the government since the 1970s. Attempts at peace have been made, but no long-term solutions have yet been found. There are many reasons why these groups want independence. One economic reason is to have control of the natural resources in a region, so that any profits made are put back into the local communities.

The transmigration policy of the Indonesian government has also caused conflict between communities. Problems arise from the loss of land and the loss of local control. Small indigenous communities can quickly become out-numbered, leading to a loss of self-identity and culture – and this can create tensions.

Conflict between the Dayaks of Kalimantan and ethnic Madurese broke out in 1997. Madurese transmigrants began arriving in Kalimantan in the 1950s. In the port town of Sampit in 2001, it is estimated between 270 and 500 Madurese, including children, were killed by groups of Dayaks. Dayaks were unhappy with the domination of the Madurese in their homeland. The population in Sampit at that time was 60 per cent Madurese. About 30,000 ethnic Madurese, even those born on Kalimantan, entered refugee camps or fled the island to Java and Madura. This placed a lot of pressure, both on the locations the refugees fled to, and on the refugees themselves, who now need to find jobs and start new lives.

A young Dayak in front of a burning Madurese house near Sampit in the 2001 violence.

Indonesia has suffered from terrorist attacks in recent years, including the Bali bombings in 2002 and 2005, the car bombs outside the Marriot Hotel in 2003, and the Australian embassy in 2004. These have been linked to Islamic extremist groups. It is very important to remember, however, that the vast majority of Indonesians do not support religious or political extremism of any sort. Extremists number only in the hundreds, at most thousands, in a population of nearly 212 million people.

Fighting began in Poso, in Sulawesi, in 1998 over local politics, transmigration pressures and the forced reallocation of land. It divided communities that previously had lived happily together along religious lines. Christians and Muslims clashed, burning down buildings and killing an estimated 2,000 people between 1999 and 2002. Tens of thousands of people fled their homes. In December 2001, the Malino Peace Accord was signed by all sides involved. Road blocks have been removed and people are tentatively going back to areas where they once lived. Reconciliation meetings, counselling, and inter-faith volleyball matches are arranged by local communities in association with the government, United Nations agencies and non-governmental organisations (NGOs). Tension is still high, but people are making a strong effort to reconcile differences and live together again peacefully.

DAILY LIFE

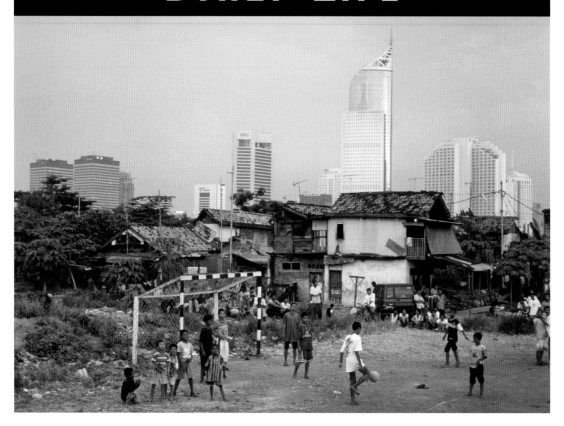

Rich and poor: unequal neighbours in Jakarta.

There are major differences in the daily lives of people in Indonesia. Culture, religion, location and wealth are all major factors. Poverty is widespread, with the gap between the richest and poorest growing. Basic services are lacking in rural areas, and many who move to the cities for paid employment often find themselves living in the cramped kampungs (densely packed districts, housing mainly poor people).

Poverty is still a major concern in Indonesia. In 2002, more than half the population lived on less than the equivalent of US$2 a day. Many more live near the poverty line and are called the marginal poor. These people are very vulnerable to entering poverty. A family illness, the loss of a job, or having to look after another relative, can send these people falling well below the poverty line. The government is making efforts to reduce the number of people in poverty, but this is made more difficult by rising unemployment.

The differences between the rich and poor are very evident in Indonesia. Kampungs often lie between rich neighbourhoods. For example, in the middle of Jakarta, a 2-metre fence separates the 5-star international Shangri La hotel from the Karet Tensin kampung. Kampungs are often located next to polluted canals and streams, lacking basic services. Without sanitation and clean water these places suffer from high levels of water-borne diseases. The quality of the housing is much worse compared to the rich neighbourhoods, where the houses are luxurious by any standards. Some of these wealthy communities have secure gates at the entrances to stop unwanted people coming in. The city authorities have begun a Kampung Improvement Programme to provide better services to the people of the deprived areas.

Access to basic services is increasing in Indonesia. In 1990, only 71 per cent of people had access to an improved water source – this grew to 78 per cent in 2000. Access to improved sanitation still remains low, only increasing from 47 per cent in 1990 to 55 per cent in 2000. Access to basic services is even lower when comparing rural and urban areas. Only 69 per cent of rural inhabitants, compared with 90 per cent of urban dwellers, had access to an improved water source.

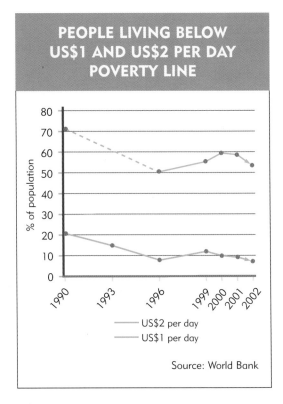

PEOPLE LIVING BELOW US$1 AND US$2 PER DAY POVERTY LINE

% of population

US$2 per day
US$1 per day

Source: World Bank

CASE STUDY
WATER IN THE MARUNDA KAMPUNG

Marunda is a kampung in Jakarta, which houses about 20,000 people. It was forced to relocate in 1984 to the north-east of the city as the original area began to be developed. The move left Marunda without a source of water or sanitation, and this created many health problems for the community. As part of the Kampung Improvement Programme, the city authorities, along with the British company Thames Water, began a £60,000 project to improve access to water and sanitation. The project began in 1999 and worked with 2,000 local people. By 2000, mains water had been connected directly to 1,600 homes and 12,000 people had access to clean water.

These workers are digging a trench for a new water pipe, as part of the Kampung Improvement Programme in Marunda, Jakarta.

HEALTH

Indonesia has been successful in lowering the under-five mortality rate by almost five times from 1960 to 2002. Also, life expectancy has increased by 25 years – from 41 in 1960, to 66 in 2001. This has been as a result of better sanitation and access to clean water, improved diets, national vaccination programmes and improved healthcare. However, there is still

LIFE EXPECTANCY AT BIRTH

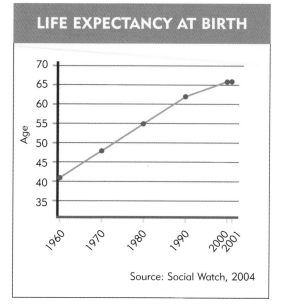

Source: Social Watch, 2004

UNDER-FIVE MORTALITY RATE (DEATHS PER 1,000 BIRTHS)

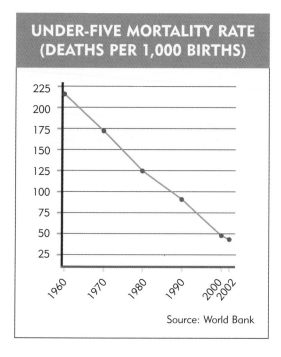

Source: World Bank

a long way to go to match the levels of many developed nations. Only 55.8 per cent of mothers giving birth have a skilled health worker present, and they are almost 21 times more likely to die whilst having their baby than women in the UK. Access to medical facilities and staff is much easier in urban than rural areas.

Indonesia has many health problems it is trying to tackle, such as malaria and tuberculosis. In 2003, the health authorities responded quickly to the outbreak of SARS

KRETEK CIGARETTES

Smoking is a popular habit for 59 per cent of male Indonesians – only 4 per cent of women smoke. Indonesians do not simply smoke tobacco. Instead, they mix the tobacco with cloves, which are then usually wrapped in corn husks to make kretek cigarettes. These are much higher in nicotine and tar than ordinary cigarettes so the health risks are greater.

Women hand-rolling Kretek cigarettes.

The challenge is to enable these primary school children to complete their full education.

(severe acute respiratory syndrome) to minimise the devastating impact the virus had caused in China and other areas of South-east Asia. HIV/AIDS amongst injecting drug users is increasingly becoming a concern for international organisations. At the moment, the level of HIV is less than 0.1 per cent of the population, but this could easily rise if nothing is done to prevent the spread of the disease.

Indoor pollution is a major health problem, with half of all Indonesian homes burning biomass fuels – such as wood, charcoal, and animal droppings – to cook with. It causes respiratory problems and it has been linked to low birth weights of babies and some types of cancer.

EDUCATION

Education improved during the Suharto period, and continues to do so today. In 2002, literacy rates for the whole population reached 83 per cent for women and 92 per cent for men. However, with conflict and a neglect of facilities, 30 per cent of primary

schools in Indonesia have been destroyed, or are beyond repair. In Aceh, for example, many children have to be taught in tents or mosques instead.

Education for Indonesian children is compulsory for nine years, but the reality is very different. Whilst enrolment rates for primary schools are high, three in every four children will not start or complete secondary school. There are immense economic pressures for older children to find paid employment to help support their families, or to tend crops on family land. Keeping children in education can be difficult for poorer families.

Private schools are popular with those who can afford the fees. Christian schools have a very high reputation, and accept children of other faiths. In 2003, it became the law that each pupil must be taught about their own religion in every Indonesian school – for example, Muslim children in Christian schools are taught about Islam.

RELIGION

When Indonesia gained independence, one of the country's guiding principles was the belief in a supreme god. People could freely choose their official religion, even if they did not practise it, as long as it was either Islam, Hinduism, Buddhism, Confucianism or Christianity. Christianity is the newest of these religions in the archipelago – arriving with the Portuguese. However, other religions have since been acknowledged, such as the Toraja religion in 1969 and the Dayak religion, Kaharigan, in 1983.

Indonesia is home to the world's largest Muslim population. Here, practising Muslims are called *santri*. For many Muslim families the

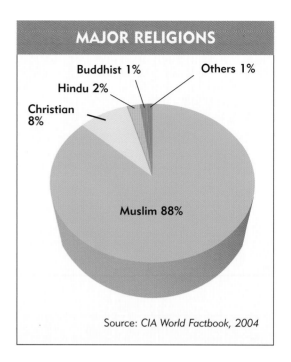

MAJOR RELIGIONS

- Buddhist 1%
- Others 1%
- Hindu 2%
- Christian 8%
- Muslim 88%

Source: *CIA World Factbook, 2004*

The festival of Nyepi is especially important for Balinese Hindus, marking the end of the old year and the beginning of the new. The day before Nyepi, there are big celebrations and lots of activity. In the evening, evil spirits are chased away by loud noise, flaming torches and bonfires. On the day of Nyepi, people do nothing. This is so that when the evil spirits come down, they think Bali is deserted and move elsewhere. This brings prosperity for the new year.

The *ogoh-ogoh* effigy is burnt on bonfires in the evening before Nyepi.

mosque provides more than a place of worship. It is a place where social organisations meet, children are taught Arabic and religious studies, and charitable donations are distributed to the poor. Many of the Islamic customs in Indonesia differ from those in some other Islamic countries – creating greater social freedoms, especially for women. Although Islam and Islamic groups have played important roles in politics Indonesia continues to be a secular (non-religious) state.

The island of Bali is mainly Hindu. It differs from Indian or Nepali Hinduism as the Balinese Hindus have a supreme god called Sanghyang Widi. Balinese gods and spirits have daily importance as offerings are made for good fortune and luck. There is a caste system, but its main significance is in religious roles and rituals, rather than the division of labour as in India.

Animism, the worship of spirits and ancestors, is still widespread in Indonesia. It remains the dominant form of worship in isolated regions of Kalimantan, in Papua and Samba. In other areas, it continues to form the basis of many people's daily lives, regardless of their religion.

WOMEN'S LIVES

Women have essential roles within Indonesian life beyond traditional family responsibilities. Women have always been active in agriculture – though often this has been for subsistence and not paid employment. The female economic contribution to the family has often been underestimated, with women having a long history of producing and selling goods in markets. Today, women are becoming better educated with more entering the labour force, especially in manufacturing industries. Women are getting married later and, in Java especially, are older when they start having children.

FEMALE LABOUR FORCE

% of total labour force — values: 50, 45, 40, 35, 30, 25, 20

Years: 1965, 1975, 1985, 1995, 2000, 2001

Source: Social Watch, 2004

Megawati Sukarnoputri became the first female president of Indonesia in 2001.

FOOD

Rice is the main staple food for much of Indonesia. Plain rice is usually cooked in the morning, along with three or four other dishes. These are left in the home for people to eat throughout the day. Chilli sauce called *sambal* accompanies most meals. Most people eat with their right hand and not with utensils as they do in other parts of the world. Indonesians are famous for their continual eating throughout the day, rather than eating just two or three larger meals. Many people can be seen enjoying *sate* (grilled meat on bamboo skewers), *gado gado* (vegetable salad with peanut sauce) and other dishes, which they buy from street vendors during the day.

As you head further east and the land becomes less fertile and drier, cassava and taro (root vegetables), sago and corn replace rice as the staple foodstuff. Throughout the islands, fish and seafood provide an important source of protein.

There are a great variety of local specialities throughout the islands – some, like bats in chilli, are a little more unusual than others.

RECREATION

Badminton is one of the most popular sports in Indonesia. The national team is very successful in international competitions. Many Indonesians follow regional and international football teams. Often in the evenings, after work or school, people can be seen playing badminton or football on the streets. Indonesia also has its own martial art called *pencak silat*, which is most popular in Sumatra and Java. Areas which have histories of tribal warfare often have traditional fighting contests and demonstrations at festivals and special ceremonies.

Indonesia has a strong tradition of music, dance and theatre. The traditional *gamelan* orchestras are made up of percussion

People stop to buy a snack from the *sate* sellers at the roadside in Yogyakarta.

Dynamic players in a match held in Jakarta.

CASE STUDY
SEPAK TAKRAW

Also known as *sepak raga*, the game of *sepak takraw* is played throughout South-east Asia, mainly by men. It is a spectacular mix of volleyball and football played with a rattan ball.

Players dive around the court to keep the ball off the ground, trying to return it over the high net. They are not allowed to use their hands, except to drop the ball onto the foot to serve. Players launch themselves up into the air to perform amazing kicks in an attempt to win a point.

instruments, such as metal gongs and drums, along with flutes and xylophones. *Dangdut* is a form of Indonesian music, often about love and romance, which mixes the *gamelan* with modern music.

Dance ranges from the nightclubs of Jakarta or Kuta, to the Mandua dance with knives in Kalimantan, or the ballet in Yogyakarta. Dance and drama are closely related with many dances telling stories. The quest of Prince Rama to find his kidnapped wife is told in the *Ramayana* dances. This is also a popular story for *wayang* puppetry. The leather shadow puppets – *wayang kulit* – are made from the hides of water buffalos. The ornate wooden puppets – *wayang golek* – show the talented craft skills of people throughout Indonesia.

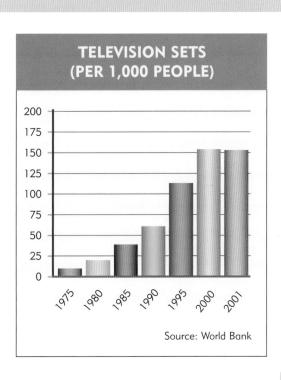

Source: World Bank

THE ENVIRONMENT

The Java rhinoceros is now endangered through poaching and habitat destruction.

I ndonesia's biodiversity (variety of plant and animal species) reflects its position between Asia and Australasia – having species from both continents. The archipelago is home to over 25 per cent of the world's fish, 17 per cent of birds, 16 per cent of reptiles and amphibians, 12 per cent of mammals and 10 per cent of all flowering plant species. But this environment is under constant threat from the many pressures of expanding industry and daily life.

BRIDGING ASIA AND AUSTRALIA

In the 1850s, the British naturalist Alfred Russel Wallace surveyed the plant and animal life in Sulawesi and Borneo. Although the two islands were close and had the same climate, he noticed they had important differences in their wildlife. In 1859, Wallace proposed the archipelago could be divided into two areas – the Asian in the west and the Australian in the east. Wallace's Line (see the map opposite) marked the boundary between the two – heading from south of the Philippines between Borneo and Sulawesi, and dividing Bali and Lombok. Further surveys have created other lines dividing the islands' wildlife, such as Weber's Line and Lydekker's Line. Weber's Line was intended to replace Wallace's Line, while Lydekker's Line, which runs around Papua, is seen as the boundary of marsupials. Sulawesi, Maluku and Nusa Tengarra are seen as a transition area between the wildlife of the two continents, sometimes called Wallacea.

On the savannah plains of Papua, bush wallabies are found, and in its vast forests there are four species of tree kangaroos. Echidnas and other marsupial animals all make Papua their home. The birdwing butterfly lives on Papua, and with a wing-span of 33cm, it is the largest butterfly in South-east Asia. Amazingly, half of all the plants and animals found in Papua are not found anywhere outside of the island of New Guinea.

On the islands of Sumatra, Borneo and Java, there are many animal species related to mainland Asia. Tigers, elephants, rhinoceroses and leopards still exist, but in declining numbers. Land use has changed over time, reducing the area covered by forest, especially on densely populated Java. Sumatra and Borneo are home to the orang-utan, the only great ape found outside of Africa. Many conservation projects are trying to increase populations of endangered species.

NUMBER OF SPECIES IN INDONESIA, 2002

	NUMBER OF SPECIES	NUMBER OF SPECIES THREATENED
Mammals	515	147
Birds*	929	114
Flowering plants	29,375	384

* = with breeding range in Indonesia

WALLACE'S, WEBER'S AND LYDEKKER'S LINES

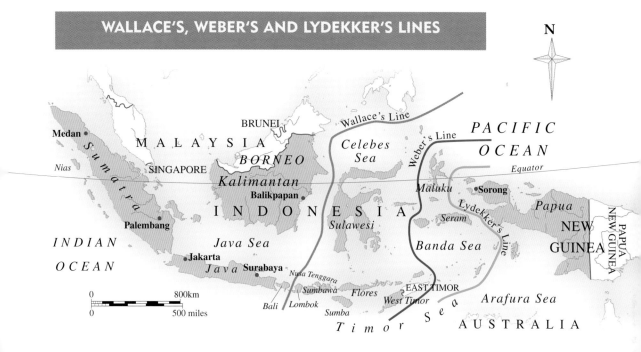

INDONESIA'S GIANT FLOWERS

Indonesia is home to a variety of giant flowers. The *Rafflesia arnoldi* is the world's largest single flower, growing up to a width of 1m. It is a parasitic plant, taking its nutrients from the plants on which it grows. The *Amorphophallus titanium* is the world's largest individual flower cluster. The plant only blooms every three to four years and can reach 3.3m tall. Both of these plants have a foul smell of decaying flesh once they are in full bloom.

The *Rafflesia arnoldi* blooms between August and November.

COASTAL AND MARINE ENVIRONMENTS

Indonesia is home to 30 per cent of the world's mangrove forests, with over 33 species of mangroves. Around Merauke on Papua, these swamps extend for 300km inland from the coast. The proboscis monkey, one of the many primates in Indonesia, inhabits the coastal forests of Kalimantan and Sumatra. It is very distinctive with its large bulbous nose.

Along with the Philippines and Malaysia, Indonesia forms part of the Coral Triangle – a region with one of the most diverse and important coastal and marine ecosystems. In Indonesian waters alone there are over 400 different species of coral. The reefs are home to some of the most beautiful fish in the world, including the clownfish, damselfish, wrasse and *Corius aygula*. Many of these are caught and sold abroad – to supply the demand for exotic and ornamental fish. The red and golden-red Asian Bonytonhue (also called Arowana) was the most wanted ornamental fish for collectors, and prices could reach thousands of pounds. The trade in this fish was banned worldwide in 1975, and they became a protected species in Indonesia in 1980. Pearl oysters are found in Indonesia, and are highly valued for their large size and high quality.

Five of the seven species of turtles are found in Indonesian waters – the leatherback, Olive Ridley, loggerhead, hawksbill and green. Green turtles have been heavily exploited, with eggs taken and turtles killed for their meat and shells. There are also 22 species of marine mammals. Dolphin-watching, off the north coast of Bali, is becoming a popular activity for tourists. This form of eco-tourism provides an important income for many local people, whilst encouraging the preservation of the ecosystem through sustainable use.

Local fishermen take tourists dolphin-watching in Bali to earn extra money.

The islands of Komodo, Padar and Rinca are home to the world's largest lizard. It is called the ora by locals, but is more commonly known as the Komodo dragon. It is a protected species and the national animal of Indonesia. Komodo dragons can grow up to 3m long and weigh over 70kg. To avoid being eaten the young live in trees, until they are too large, after which they find holes to shelter in.

Komodo dragons like to eat dead or decaying flesh – preferring the Timor deer – but they are not really fussy and will even eat each other. They often ambush prey, killing them with their strong claws and sharp teeth. With septic saliva, the prey is likely to die from blood poisoning within a week, if not killed outright. At one go, the Komodo dragon is able to eat up to 80 per cent of its body weight. This is important, as they are opportunist feeders – if there is no food then they can go for days without eating. Large meals can take up to a week to digest.

Workers stand on illegally sawn timber. Illegal logging is destroying the Indonesian forests.

THREATS TO THE ENVIRONMENT

Indonesia faces a range of threats to the environment through the changing uses of the land, and the misuse and overuse of resources. Illegal logging is a major problem, with deforestation measured at an average of 13,124km^2 per year between 1990 and 2000.

The mining of coral and coral rocks for cement and the construction industry is destroying the reefs, which provide a natural defence against the sea – so rates of coastal erosion are climbing fast. In Candidasa in Bali, the beach disappeared with the destruction of the reef.

The marine and coastal ecosystems are also under threat from unsustainable fishing practices. Blast fishing, cyanide fishing, the use of traps and reef gleaning all destroy coral and the habitat for fish. Over-fishing has seen stock numbers rapidly decline. Water pollution, including untreated waste, can smother the corals and kill them.

POSITIVE SOLUTIONS

There are a number of positive steps, which have been taken at the local, national and international level to protect the environment. There are 373,200km^2 of national protected land – 20.6 per cent of the total land area – an increase from 7.6 per cent in 1985. National parks and marine reserves not only offer protection to the diverse species of Indonesia, they also provide an opportunity for research and eco-tourism. Orang-utan conservation in Kalimantan and Sumatra is one such example.

The government has also taken steps to reduce the destructive impact of industries. The reduction in logging areas, limiting open-cast mining and banning the clearing of land by fire, are three examples.

International pressure can help promote sustainable use of materials within Indonesia. In early 2004, the British government banned the importing of plywood from Indonesia, as it was reported that 80 per cent was produced from illegally logged trees. This had the immediate effect of the Indonesian government inspecting and issuing licences to those factories using only legal materials.

KALIMANTAN FOREST FIRES

Fires raged out of control in Kalimantan in 1997, and again in 1998. A haze developed over the island, spreading to Singapore and Malaysia. Fires used to clear land by plantation owners and indigenous groups, who use swidden (slash-and-burn) agriculture, got out of control. This was made worse by the effects of El Niño, which caused unusually dry conditions. The fires caused widespread damage to the environment and increased respiratory illnesses amongst people affected by the haze.

CASE STUDY
GUNUNG LEUSER NATIONAL PARK

Increasing orang-utan numbers will be slow and difficult as adult females produce few young.

The Gunung Leuser National Park in northern Sumatra is home to the endangered Sumatran species of rhinoceros, tiger and orang-utan. Many people believe this is the last place in Sumatra where wild populations of these species can be increased through conservation projects.

The region is under threat – illegal logging is destroying habitats and causing an increase in mudslides as the protective canopy has been lost. Illegal logging, mudslides and adverse weather conditions have been attributed to the flash flooding of Bukit Lawang, on the edge of the national park in 2003 – over 200 people were killed. A major road-building project, linking Aceh with the rest of Sumatra, threatens to destroy more of the national park.

NATIONAL PARKS

🍄 National park

🦪 National marine park

PACIFIC OCEAN

N

Medan

BRUNEI

Celebes Sea

Gunung Leuser National Park

MALAYSIA

SINGAPORE

Equator

Kalimantan

Sorong

INDONESIA

Papua

PAPUA NEW GUINEA

Palembang

Java Sea

Banda Sea

INDIAN OCEAN

Jakarta

Surabaya

EAST TIMOR

Arafura Sea

0   800km
0   500 miles

Komodo National Park

Timor Sea

AUSTRALIA

Scavenging for items in the waste dumped in an Indonesian river.

INDUSTRIAL AND URBAN POLLUTION

Pollution is a major problem in Indonesia. Respiratory diseases are the sixth largest cause of death in the country, and many of these could be avoided if air pollution was reduced. Urban areas tend to be the worst affected, as industries and motor vehicles are most concentrated here. Between 1995 and 2000, the number of vehicles in Indonesia increased from 12 million to almost 21 million, and the numbers keep rising. Carbon dioxide emissions, which are linked with global warming, have increased by over 271 per cent since 1980, with 87.1 million tonnes produced in 2001. Much of these emissions come from generating power for both industry and domestic use. Almost 87 per cent of energy in Indonesia is produced by the burning of fossil fuels (gas 34 per cent, coal 29 per cent and oil 24 per cent). Air pollution is set to get worse if renewable sources are not used. At the moment, only 4 per cent of Indonesia's massive geothermal potential is being harnessed.

The government is trying to ban lead petrol throughout Indonesia to cut lead pollution. However, the state-owned oil company Pertamina does not yet have the capabilities to produce enough unleaded fuel – since the economic crisis there has been a lack of funding for the necessary upgrading of the refineries.

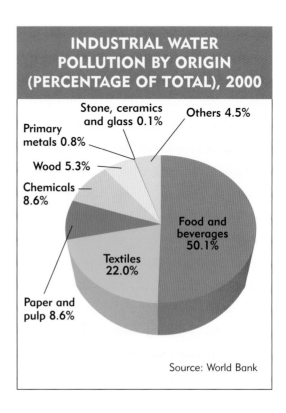

INDUSTRIAL WATER POLLUTION BY ORIGIN (PERCENTAGE OF TOTAL), 2000

- Stone, ceramics and glass 0.1%
- Others 4.5%
- Primary metals 0.8%
- Wood 5.3%
- Chemicals 8.6%
- Food and beverages 50.1%
- Textiles 22.0%
- Paper and pulp 8.6%

Source: World Bank

Indonesia uses around 75 billion cubic metres of water a year, which is taken from the rivers, lakes and underground reservoirs. The widespread use of unregulated agricultural chemicals is causing serious ecological damage as these find their way into larger ecosystems. Many factories have been reportedly dumping untreated waste materials into local rivers.

Although sanitation is improving in many areas, the level of water contamination caused by sewage is high. A study in Jakarta found 90 per cent of the shallow ground water wells were polluted with domestic waste in 2001. Sea water contaminating drinking water supplies is a major problem in coastal towns and cities as the local water table lowers due to overuse.

CASE STUDY
TRAFFIC POLLUTION IN JAKARTA

Jakarta has one of the most polluted atmospheres in the world. Many of the 5 million vehicles in the city are scooters and motorcycles without catalytic converters, which lower harmful emissions. Lead pollution is a problem. In one study, a third of children had levels of lead in their blood high enough to cause learning and concentration problems. Unleaded petrol is being phased in throughout Indonesia and more rapidly in Jakarta. But the city authorities only have the power to enforce these regulations with public vehicles, which account for little over 6 per cent of Jakarta's traffic.

The authorities introduced a 'three-in-one' policy, which required each car to have at least three people in it when driving into the city centre. It has not been very successful in cutting the number of cars. Instead, many Indonesians make money from it. They line the roads leading into the centre and drivers without enough passengers pick them up and pay them for the short trip into the controlled area.

Measures need to be stepped up to reduce pollution within Jakarta.

LOOKING AHEAD

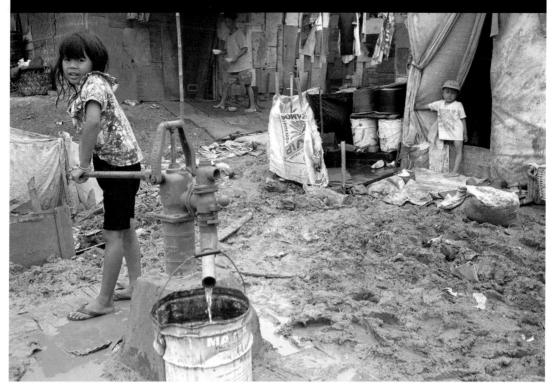

Poverty and the lack of basic services continue to be major problems.

I ndonesia is a spectacular country, diverse in landscape and people. It has amazing potential to grow into a wealthy and prosperous nation. Yet it faces many challenges on the road ahead. The questions of national unity, the control of natural resources, the importance of the environment and the need to reduce poverty all face the country.

REGIONAL QUESTIONS

'Unity in diversity' or *bhinneka tunggal ika* (see page 30) as they say in Indonesia, is being tested. Since the mid-1970s, the government in Jakarta has been facing calls for independence in distant provinces, including Aceh in Sumatra, and Papua. Independence has not been granted and violent confrontation has continued. Efforts at finding peace have not led to any long-term solutions.

The government recently started a programme of decentralisation. This gives greater powers to regional, provincial and district level decision makers over everyday issues. It is hoped this will reduce conflict as people work together on improving conditions in their areas. Supporters of decentralisation argue it extends democracy, involving more people in decision making.

On the other hand, there are many people who are opposed to regional autonomy and decentralisation. Some say there are not enough resources and qualified people to run the extra layers of government. Others argue the rampant corruption which plagues Indonesia will only increase. Small powerful groups will dominate councils, using them to further their own interests. Violence has already occurred due to unrepresentative local politics and decentralisation may increase conflict.

There is also the issue of who controls what resources. Not all areas in Indonesia have access to the same raw materials or size of workforce. Many people fear there will be a growing division between resource-rich areas and those areas without. President Yudhoyono faces a very difficult job in stamping out corruption and maintaining a unified nation.

POVERTY AND INEQUALITY

There are vast differences in wealth in Indonesia and access to resources. Whilst the number of people using the Internet is increasing, almost half the population is still without electricity. Access to basic services, such as sanitation, would improve the quality of life for large numbers of people. Drinking water would not become infected and people would suffer less diarrhoeal diseases. These diseases are still a major cause of death in Indonesia.

If poverty can be reduced further, then Indonesia's potential has a greater chance of being fulfilled. One of the problems with poverty is that it often forces children out of school. Education is crucial, especially if the country wants to develop more highly skilled jobs in new sectors of industry, which will help the economy grow.

TELECOMMUNICATIONS DATA, 2002 (PER 1,000 PEOPLE)

Mainline phones	37
Mobile phones	55
Internet users	38

Source: World Bank

THE ECONOMY

The Indonesian economy is beginning to grow after the crisis in 1997, but it is vulnerable to changes in the global economy. International agreements have in the past protected Indonesian industries. With some of these agreements ending – for example, for textiles – unemployment is set to increase as Indonesia cannot keep up with other competitors. Indonesia needs to increase the range of products and services it supplies to remain internationally competitive. Tourism has a major potential to provide new jobs and economic growth.

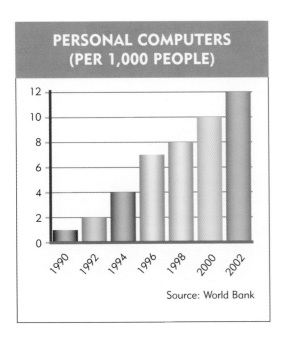

PERSONAL COMPUTERS (PER 1,000 PEOPLE)

Source: World Bank

Internet use is increasing within Indonesia, mainly in the cities.

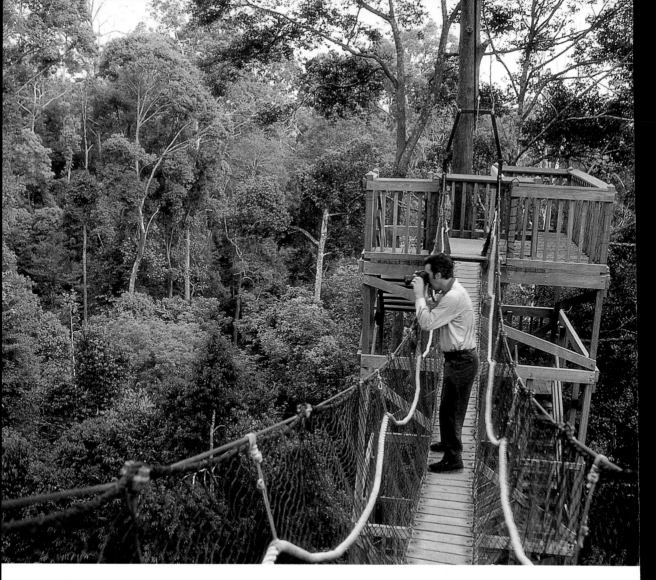

BALANCING THE ECONOMY AND THE ENVIRONMENT

Expanding eco-tourism supports the economy, whilst protecting the environment.

The big question which faces Indonesia is how best to use the country's natural resources to improve people's standard of living, whilst protecting the environment. It is not an easy situation, and is one facing many developing countries. There are often compromises made between people and the environment, and it is essential a balance is reached – protecting globally important ecosystems and improving people's quality of life.

Sustainable management of resources is needed, but it is more than passing laws saying how much forest can be cleared, or what practices can be used. There needs to be enforcement, otherwise the illegal logging and fishing will destroy ecosystems that have developed over millions of years. Renewable sources need to be managed sensibly – with the long-term goal being the ability to continually use them.

Indonesia has a huge potential to expand geothermal, hydroelectric (HEP) and solar energy production. Lowering the dependency on fossil fuels will help reduce the growing carbon dioxide emissions, which are linked with global warming, and cut pollution. It is a critical time for the environment and unity of the archipelago. Wasted chances could turn a bright future bleak.

THE UNKNOWN

Not all the events which affect Indonesia can be controlled. It is an archipelago of volcanoes and geological instability. The active volcanoes are monitored and plans are in place to evacuate people close to these, if necessary. However, homes and livelihoods cannot be evacuated, and these can be wiped out with one blast. The Asian tsunami on 26 December 2004 and the earthquake off the island of Nias on 28 March 2005 demonstrated not everything can be predicted and devastation only takes minutes. Nature's power has, and can again in the future, create major obstacles to be overcome on the development pathway for Indonesia.

CASE STUDY
THE ASIAN TSUNAMI:
DESTRUCTION AND RECONSTRUCTION

Within minutes towns were flattened, lives lost and the livelihoods of those remaining were destroyed by the giant waves caused by the earthquake kilometres off the Sumatran coast on 26 December 2004. The north tip and west coast of Sumatra were devastated. Over 125,000 people were confirmed dead. Tens of thousands more are missing, presumed dead, in what has been described as one of the worst humanitarian disasters in modern times.

Aceh was hit the hardest by the tsunami. It is, however, not a simple question of nature's destructive power. The ability to respond to the crisis and to rebuild lives after the event is shaped by social and political forces. Aceh has seen violent conflict between the Indonesian military and separatist groups – which has taken about 13,000 lives since 1976. Concern for the safety of relief workers initially caused the military to limit the movement of aid organisations. After a ceasefire was reached, relief efforts are now occurring throughout the province. The question remains whether or not the issues which have caused the conflict can be resolved without the return to violence.

Poverty and unemployment are exceptionally high in the wake of the tsunami, but money has been donated to reconstruct infrastructure, towns and livelihoods. Corruption threatens to take those essential funds away from the people who need it most. How quickly and successfully corruption is tackled will shape the future of Aceh and the rest of Indonesia – for the better or worse.

Standing amongst the devastation in Aceh. The challenges of reconstruction lay ahead.

GLOSSARY

Arable land Land in use for temporary crops, meadow, pasture or deliberately left fallow. It does not include land abandoned as a result of swidden agriculture.

Archipelago A group of islands.

Autonomy The ability for people to govern more of their local affairs in their communities, rather than everything being decided by the central government.

Blast Fishing The use of explosives to stun fish so they are easier to catch. This practice destroys coral reefs.

Continental shelf A section of the continental land area found below sea level. The shelf is flat, or very gently sloping, forming an extension to the coastal plain. There is a sheer drop at the edge of the shelf where it meets deep ocean.

Cyanide fishing A fishing method which uses cyanide, a poison, to tranquilise fish. The poison damages the coral and the marine ecosystem.

Decentralisation The process by which the government gives more power to the provinces and districts to look after their own affairs.

Ecosystem The relationship between interacting living organisms and their physical environment. An ecosystem can be small, like a stream, or large like planet Earth.

Eco-tourism Tourism that is sensitive to its impact on the environment and people.

El Niño An upwelling of warm water in the tropical Pacific Ocean, which affects the weather patterns, generally bringing unusually dry weather. It usually occurs once in every four to eight years.

GDP (Gross Domestic Product) The monetary value of goods and services produced by a country in a year.

Geothermal power Energy gained from the internal heat of the Earth. Volcanoes and hot springs are great sources of this energy, which can be used to produce electricity.

GNI (Gross National Income) The monetary value of goods and services produced by a country, plus any income from earnings overseas by the country's citizens, in a single year. It used to be called Gross National Product (GNP).

Improved sanitation Disposal facilities for human waste that are secure and prevent humans, animals and insects contacting the waste.

Improved water source Water that comes from a direct connection to a household, a public standpipe, bore hole, protected well or spring or secure rainwater collection. The source must be within 1km of where a person lives. It does not include unsecured wells, vendors or tanker trucks.

Irrigate To deliberately supply farmland with water. This includes controlled flooding, which is used for wet-rice cultivation for example.

Kampung The word means village, but it is used to describe small settlements usually of poor housing in deprived areas.

Marginal poor Describes the group of people who have an income just above the poverty line. These people could easily fall below the line if changes happen in their lives, such as illness or the loss of a job.

Militia A non-government military force.

Naturalist An expert in the natural history of plants and animals.

Ocean trench A large, linear depression formed in the ocean floor where subduction of tectonic plates occurs. They are usually 50 to 100km wide, and several thousand metres deep.

Ousted Forced to resign from a position by other people.

Permanent cropland Land that is used for crops that occupy the land for long periods of time and do not need to be replanted after each harvest. Coffee, cocoa and rubber are all examples of such crops.

Population density The number of people living in a certain area of land.

Poverty line A measurement of poverty. All the people who have a daily income less than a certain value, for example US$1, are said to be below the poverty line.

Purchasing Power Parity (PPP) The calculation made to some national statistics so they can be compared with other countries accurately.

Reconciliation Finding a peaceful understanding of differences between individuals and groups.

Reef gleaning A destructive method of fishing that involves using tools to scrape away coral to gain access to fish and other marine animals. It creates large areas of dead reef.

Relative humidity The ratio of the moisture the air contains to the amount of moisture the air could hold at a certain temperature, expressed as a percentage.

Separatists A group of people who want independence from a country so they can form their own nation.

Services Economic activities that are paid for, although no physical product is made. This includes tourism, banking, health and education.

Subduction The movement of one tectonic plate underneath another one as they move towards each other.

Subsistence The production of enough food and other goods to meet the needs of the household without producing excess which could be sold.

Sustainable Methods used to make sure something continues to exist, or happen, for a long time.

Swidden agriculture (slash-and-burning) Land is cleared and the debris is burnt so it can be used to grow crops. Once the farming of the land is finished it is left to regenerate naturally.

Tectonic plates Large sections of the Earth's crust which move slowly over the Earth's molten mantle.

Transmigration (*transmigrasi*) The policy of moving people from a densely populated area to one which is less populated.

Tsunami Giant waves caused by volcanic eruptions or other movements in the Earth's surface, such as undersea earthquakes.

FURTHER INFORMATION

BOOKS TO READ:
Historical Atlas of Indonesia by Robert Cribb (University of Hawaii Press, 2000) Useful beginning chapters on the changing geology and landscape of the archipelago with lots of illustrative maps.

Wild Indonesia: The Wildlife and Scenery of the Indonesian Archipelago by Gerald Cubitt, Tony and Jane Whitten (New Holland, 1992) Beautiful photographs of the plants and animals of Indonesia.

Sulawesi Seas: Indonesia's Magnificent Underwater Realm by Mike Severns (Staples Ecenberger Publishing, 1994) Looks at the marine ecosystem of Indonesia, illustrated with stunning photographs.

Lonely Planet Guide: Indonesia by Mark Elliott, Paul Greenway, Virginia Jealous and others (Lonely Planet, 2003) A comprehensive guide to travelling in Indonesia.

WEBSITES:
GENERAL INFORMATION AND STATISTICS
Indonesian Embassy
http://www.indonesianembassy.org.uk
Introductory information on Indonesia with links to other Indonesian-based websites.

Indonesian Central Bureau of Statistics
http://www.bps.go.id/
Official statistics on Indonesia.

Foreign and Commonwealth Office
http://www.fco.gov.uk
Brief introduction and updated information on countries of the world including Indonesia and East Timor.

CIA World Factbook
http://www.cia.gov/cia/publications/factbook/geos/id.html
The page on Indonesia contains lots of facts and analysis.

DEVELOPMENT
United Nations Development Programme
http://www.undp.or.id/
Includes information on international projects in Indonesia.

WILDLIFE AND NATIONAL PARKS
WWF (World Wildlife Fund for Nature)
http://wwf.org/
You can link to the Indonesian website as well as the British website, which is easier to search.

Komodo National Park
http://www.komodonationalpark.org
Information on the park and species that live in it.

Sumatran Orang-utan Society
http://orangutans-sos.org/
Information about the Sumatran orang-utan.

INDEX

Numbers shown in **bold** refer to pages with maps, graphic illustrations or photographs.

Casting a fishing net on the beach in Mentiggi, Lombok.